The Song of Hiawatha

by Henry Wadsworth Longfellow

abridged by Christine Hall and Martin Coles

Setting the scene

Hiawatha's grandmother was the beautiful Nokomis who fell from the moon. Early in the poem it says

> *From the full moon fell Nokomis,*
> *Fell the beautiful Nokomis ...*

Nokomis had a daughter called Wenonah who also grew up to be very beautiful.

> *And the daughter of Nokomis*
> *Grew up like the prairie lilies,*
> *Grew a tall and slender maiden,*
> *With the beauty of the moonlight,*
> *With the beauty of the starlight.*

Nokomis warned Wenonah to stay away from the West-Wind, but Wenonah fell in love with him. Wenonah and the West-Wind had a baby son called Hiawatha, "a son of love and sorrow".

The West-Wind was "false and faithless" and he left Wenonah. Wenonah died of sorrow. So Hiawatha was brought up by his grandmother, Nokomis. At the start of these extracts we see Hiawatha as a boy who loved animals and found that he could talk to them.

Hiawatha grew up to be a brave and talented man. Later in the poem we hear about one of his many adventures – with a giant, ugly fish.

Hiawatha's Childhood

... By the shores of Gitche Gumee,
By the shining Big-Sea-Water,
Stood the wigwam of Nokomis,
Daughter of the Moon, Nokomis.
Dark behind it rose the forest,
Rose the black and gloomy pine-trees,
Rose the firs with cones upon them;
Bright before it beat the water,
Beat the clear and sunny water,
Beat the shining Big-Sea-Water.

There the wrinkled old Nokomis
Nursed the little Hiawatha,
Rocked him in his linden cradle,
Bedded soft in moss and rushes,
Safely bound with reindeer sinews;
Stilled his fretful wail by saying,
"Hush! the Naked Bear will hear thee!"
Lulled him into slumber, singing,
"Ewa-yea! my little owlet!
Who is this, that lights the wigwam?
With his great eyes lights the wigwam?
Ewa-yea! my little owlet!"

linden made from a lime tree
slumber sleep

3

4

... At the door on summer evenings
Sat the little Hiawatha;
Heard the whispering of the pine-trees,
Heard the lapping of the waters,
Sounds of music, words of wonder;
"Minne-wawa!" said the pine-trees,
"Mudway-aushka!" said the water.

... When he heard the owls at midnight,
Hooting, laughing in the forest,
"What is that?" he cried in terror,
"What is that," he said, "Nokomis?"
And the good Nokomis answered:
"That is but the owl and owlet,
Talking in their native language,
Talking, scolding at each other."

scolding at telling off

5

Then the little Hiawatha
Learned of every bird its language,
Learned their names and all their secrets,
How they built their nests in Summer,
Where they hid themselves in Winter,
Talked with them whene'er he met them,
Called them "Hiawatha's Chickens".

6

Of all beasts he learned the language,
Learned their names and all their secrets,
How the beavers built their lodges,
Where the squirrels hid their acorns,
How the reindeer ran so swiftly,
Why the rabbit was so timid,
Talked with them whene'er he met them,
Called them "Hiawatha's Brothers".

lodges homes
timid shy

7

Hiawatha's Fishing

Forth upon the Gitche Gumee,
On the shining Big-Sea-Water,
With his fishing-line of cedar,
Of the twisted bark of cedar,
Forth to catch the sturgeon Nahma,
Mishe-Nahma, King of Fishes,
In his birch canoe exulting
All alone went Hiawatha.

Through the clear, transparent water
He could see the fishes swimming
Far down in the depths below him;
See the yellow perch, the Sahwa,
Like a sunbeam in the water,
See the Shawgashee, the craw-fish,
Like a spider on the bottom,
On the white and sandy bottom.

forth forward
sturgeon a type of fish
exulting happy

8

At the stern sat Hiawatha,
With his fishing-line of cedar;
In his plumes the breeze of morning
Played as in the hemlock branches;
On the bow, with tail erected,
Sat the squirrel, Adjidaumo;
In his fur the breeze of morning
Played as in the prairie grasses.

stern back of the boat
plumes feathers
hemlock a kind of tree
bow front of the boat
prairie open grassy land

On the white sand of the bottom

Lay the monster Mishe-Nahma,

Lay the sturgeon, King of Fishes;

Through his gills he breathed the water,

With his fins he fanned and winnowed,

With his tail he swept the sand-floor.

winnowed beat

There he lay in all his armour;
On each side a shield to guard him,
Plates of bone upon his forehead,
Down his sides and back and shoulders
Plates of bone with spines projecting
Painted was he with his war-paints,
Stripes of yellow, red, and azure,
Spots of brown and spots of sable;
And he lay there on the bottom,
Fanning with his fins of purple,
As above him Hiawatha
In his birch canoe came sailing,
With his fishing-line of cedar.

azure blue
sable black

12

"Take my bait," cried Hiawatha,
Down into the depths beneath him,
"Take my bait, O Sturgeon, Nahma!
Come up from below the water,
Let us see which is the stronger!"
And he dropped his line of cedar
Through the clear, transparent water,
Waited vainly for an answer,
Long sat waiting for an answer,
And repeating loud and louder,
"Take my bait, O King of Fishes!"

vainly without success

Quiet lay the sturgeon, Nahma,
Fanning slowly in the water,
Looking up at Hiawatha,
Listening to his call and clamour,
His unnecessary tumult,
Till he wearied of the shouting ...

clamour *shouting*
tumult *noise*
wearied *grew tired*

14

... And again the sturgeon, Nahma,
Heard the shout of Hiawatha,
Heard his challenge of defiance,
The unnecessary tumult,
Ringing far across the water.

defiance *standing up against someone*

From the white sand of the bottom
Up he rose with angry gesture,
Quivering in each nerve and fibre,
Clashing all his plates of armour,
Gleaming bright with all his war-paint;
In his wrath he darted upward,
Flashing leaped into the sunshine,
Opened his great jaws, and swallowed
Both canoe and Hiawatha.

wrath anger

Down into that darksome cavern
            the   Hiawatha,
As a log on some black river
Shoots and plunges down the rapids,
Found himself in utter darkness,
Groped about in helpless wonder,
Till he felt a great heart beating,
Throbbing in that utter darkness.

plunged dived
headlong head-first

17

And he smote it in his anger,
With his fist, the heart of Nahma,
Felt the mighty King of Fishes
Shudder through each nerve and fibre,
Heard the water gurgle round him
As he leaped and staggered through it,
Sick at heart, and faint and weary.

smote hit

18

Crosswise then did Hiawatha

Drag his birch-canoe for safety,

Lest from out the jaws of Nahma,

In the turmoil and confusion,

Forth he might be hurled and perish.

And the squirrel, Adjidaumo,

Frisked and chatted very gayly,

Toiled and tugged with Hiawatha

Till the labour was completed.

lest *in case*

perish *die*

frisked *played*

toiled *worked*

labour *work*

Then said Hiawatha to him,
"O my little friend, the squirrel,
Bravely have you toiled to help me;
Take the thanks of Hiawatha,
And the name which now he gives you;
For hereafter and forever
Boys shall call you Adjidaumo,
'Tail-in-air the boys' shall call you!"

And again the sturgeon, Nahma,
Gasped and quivered in the water,
Then was still, and drifted landward
Till he grated on the pebbles,
Till the listening Hiawatha
Heard him grate upon the margin,
Felt him strand upon the pebbles,
Knew that Nahma, King of Fishes,
Lay there dead upon the margin.

landward towards land
grated scraped
margin shore
strand run aground

21

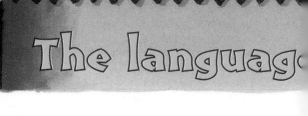

The language

- **Native American words** – for example, 'Sahwa' and 'Shawgashee' (page 9).

- **Names of people and animals** – there is often a name and a title or description, for example, 'Mishe-Nahma, King of Fishes' (page 8); 'Daughter of the Moon, Nokomis' (page 2).

- **Place names** – also have two parts to their name, for example, 'Gitche Gumee ... the shining Big-Sea-Water' (page 2).

- **Rhythm** – the poem is famous for its strong and regular rhythm.

- **Naming** animals gives them importance and dignity, for example, 'Adjidaumo, Tail-in-air'(page 20); 'Hiawatha's Chickens' (page 6).

- **Songs** - Nokomis's song is included in the poem (page 3). The songs of the natural world are also suggested by using onomatopoeia (page 4).

- **Personification** – for example, the image of the fish is like a warrior (page 12).

Henry Wadsworth Longfellow

Henry Wadsworth Longfellow was born in 1807, in Portland, Maine, U.S.A. He worked as a professor and librarian, and he loved to travel. He spoke English, French, Spanish, German and Italian and he lived in Germany for some time. He was also a keen writer, of textbooks and poetry, and he translated poetry from other languages.

Longfellow married his first wife in 1831 but she died in 1835. He took a job teaching languages at Harvard, a famous American university. He married his second wife in 1843. He continued to write: travel writing, romantic novels and poems. Some of his poems spoke out against slavery.

In 1854 Longfellow gave up his teaching job at Harvard University. In 1855 he wrote *The Song of Hiawatha*. His long poems were very successful and popular with the public. In 1861, Longfellow's second wife died after her dress caught fire. After this had happened Longfellow wrote and translated more religious poetry. He died on March 24, 1882, in Cambridge, Massachusetts.

Henry Wadsworth Longfellow was one of the most popular American poets of his time.